To All
Terrarium Keepers

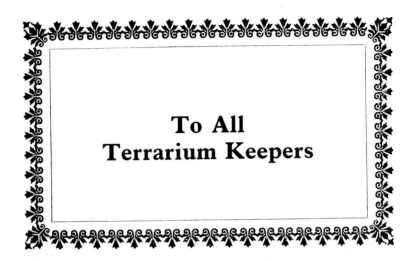

Front and back endpapers: *Though its colors seem almost unreal, more like those of gaudy plastic lawn-ornament frogs, this is a real animal. The unusual tropical treefrog* Agalychnis annae *is from Costa Rica. Photo by George Dibley.*

Title page: *a "mouth with legs,"* Ceratophrys ornata. *All of the South American horned frogs are hardy inhabitants for cooler woodland terraria and will eat almost anything they can cram into their cavernous mouths, including worms, crickets, and small mice. Photo by K. T. Nemuras.*

A Beginner's Guide To
Terrariums

Written By
Richard Haas

Contents

© 1986 by T.F.H. Publications, Inc. Distributed in the UNITED STATES by T.F.H. Publications, Inc., 211 West Sylvania Avenue, Neptune City, NJ 07753; in CANADA by H & L Pet Supplies Inc., 27 Kingston Crescent, Kitchener, Ontario N2B 2T6; Rolf C. Hagen Ltd., 3225 Sartelon Street, Montreal 382 Quebec; in CANADA to the Book Trade by Macmillan of Canada (A Division of Canada Publishing Corporation), 164 Commander Boulevard, Agincourt, Ontario M1S 3C7; in ENGLAND by T.F.H. Publications Limited, 4 Kier Park, Ascot, Berkshire SL5 7DS; in AUSTRALIA AND THE SOUTH PACIFIC by T.F.H. (Australia) Pty. Ltd., Box 149, Brookvale 2100 N.S.W., Australia; in NEW ZEALAND by Ross Haines & Son, Ltd., 18 Monmouth Street, Grey Lynn, Auckland 2 New Zealand; in SINGAPORE AND MALAYSIA by MPH Distributors (S) Pte., Ltd., 601 Sims Drive, #03/07/21, Singapore 1438; in the PHILIPPINES by Bio-Research, 5 Lippay Street, San Lorenzo Village, Makati Rizal; in SOUTH AFRICA by Multipet Pty. Ltd., 30 Turners Avenue, Durban 4001. Published by T.F.H. Publications, Inc. Manufactured in the United States of America by T.F.H. Publications, Inc.

1.
Introduction

The terrarium, simply stated, is an enclosed re-creation of a small bit of a terrestrial plant-animal association as it occurs in nature. Thus, if one attempts to recreate a small bit of the great southwestern desert in a glass box

The wood frog, Rana sylvatica, *is a common woodland frog over much of North America, ranging even as far north as the Arctic Circle. It is small (2-3 inches) and makes a good pet. It can sometimes be found in great profusion when it breeds in the spring. Photo by Aaron Norman.*

Anolis equestris is an impressive lizard usually sold as a "Cuban anole." Warm tropical terraria are preferred, and, as one may guess from the expression on this specimen, large amounts of food are necessary—this species tends to become emaciated very quickly if not well-fed. Foods should consist of large insects such as crickets and roaches and "pinkie" mice. Some specimens even accept fruits such as grapes. Photo by J. Dommers.

or a section of the floor of an eastern United States deciduous forest or a tropical rain forest, one has in fact made a terrarium. The construction and maintenance of simple terrariums of various types is the scope of this book.

2.
Equipment

The most obvious piece of equipment needed for the construction of a terrarium is a suitable container. The very best and most easily obtained container is an ordinary aquarium. Many terrarium keepers use as their container old leaky aquariums that have seen better

The most economical and convenient container for a terrarium is a standard aquarium, many sizes of which are available in any pet shop. A long, low aquarium is best for many terrarium projects, but a taller one may be necessary if one intends to keep arboreal animals such as treefrogs or anoles. Photo by Dr. Herbert R. Axelrod.

days. Small leaks are not of any great consequence in most terrariums.

Other suitable containers are clear plastic shoe boxes, refrigerator boxes, or large brandy snifters (frequently available at florists already set up as tropical terrariums suitable for anoles and small tree frogs). Inexpensive desert terrariums may be constructed from sturdy wooden boxes in which a sheet of glass is substituted for one side of the box.

All terrariums must be suitably covered. For most a hardware cloth or screen top is fine. For tropical or aqua-terrarium types, a glass cover reduces water loss by evaporation. It should be placed about one-eighth of an inch above the frame of the aquarium. This reduces the possibility of overheating the terrarium if it receives direct sunlight. This separation is best accomplished by gluing a piece of thin cork or cut-up ice-cream bar sticks on each corner of the aquarium frame.

If, as many terrarium keepers do, you wish to collect your own local materials, then suitable equipment for collecting must be obtained. This varies tremendously with locale, distance from collecting areas, scope of interest, etc. Such things are trowels, shovels for collecting soil and plants, nets and nooses for collecting frogs, lizards, etc., and old pillowcases or plastic bags with holes punched in them for transport back home are the minimum requirements.

Much of the equipment and materials can be easily purchased at local aquarium or pet shops and by visits to local florists and plant nurseries. Many of the popular terrarium animals are readily available at your pet shop all year long. With increasing habitat destruction and

The spotted salamander, Ambystoma maculatum, *is an attractive large woodland salamander that feeds well in captivity, especially if offered soft-bodied invertebrates such as earthworms. Once a common species, its range has become fragmented due to development, and it is considered to be a threatened species in some states; thus, special permits may be necessary to collect or keep it. Photo by J. K. Langhammer.*

The Western Painted turtle, Chrysemys picta bellii, *is one of a series of subspecies of the genus* Chrysemys. *All are very pretty animals, particularly as hatchlings, and are very common over most of North America. They are hardy in captivity but require large amounts of vegetable matter in their diet. Especially well-suited to this purpose are leafy aquatic plants such as* Anacharis. *Photo by Dr. Herbert R. Axelrod.*

restrictions on collecting in the U.S.A. and Europe, more and more hobbyists find it easier to purchase animals rather than remove them from the local wild habitats.

3.
Setting Up

The desert terrarium

This is the easiest to establish and to maintain. All that is required to adequately house a few young tortoises (purchased, not collected, as native species are protected in the U.S.), collared lizards, or spiny lizards is a sand

Kingsnakes are highly recommended terrarium animals. Although in nature they feed on a variety of small vertebrates, most can be maintained in captivity on a diet of rodents such as mice or rats. This is a "chocolate" banded California kingsnake, Lampropeltis getulus californiae. *Photo by Ken Lucas, Steinhart Aquarium.*

13

Eublepharine geckos include species such as the North American Coleonyx *and this species, the leopard gecko,* Eublepharius macularius, *which hails from the Persian region. Unlike most geckos, eublepharines have movable eyelids and reduced toe pads. They are nocturnal desert lizards that need to be kept hot and dry. Photo by H. Hansen, Aquarium Berlin.*

bottom, and, for the lizards, a few rocks arranged so that they can climb up and sun themselves. The latter are essential. It is not true that desert reptiles can withstand great heat stress. During the heat of the day most desert reptiles hide underground in rodent burrows or under bushes, and if confined to an exposed area under the full sun they may be expected to die shortly if ground temperatures exceed 110°F. Desert reptiles (indeed, most terrestrial reptiles) maintain what for them is proper body temperature by moving in and out of the sun, alternately heating and cooling themselves and by

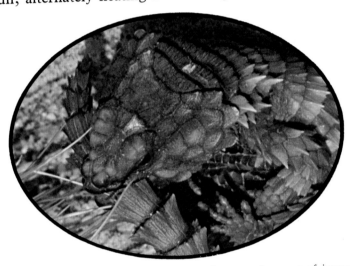

Cordylids, also known as "armadillo lizards," are another group of interesting desert lizards. Their heavily armored bodies are extremely resistant to water loss and predation, and they can even roll themselves into a spiny ball if attacked. Photo of Cordylus cataphractus by Bertrand E. Baur.

these means keeping their internal temperatures within relatively narrow ranges of optimal operating temperatures.

Thus, in preparing a desert terrarium part of it should be brightly and warmly illuminated and part in relative shade. If the terrarium is small, say, five-gallon size, a rock in the shade should be propped up to allow the animal to get under it, completely away from the light. Sand should be fine-grained and deep enough to allow the animals to bury themselves. Horned lizards, in particular, frequently bury themselves almost completely in sand. Depending on the size of the terrarium, an ordinary light bulb of from 60 to 100 watts mounted in a reflecting hood should be positioned about 5 to 12 inches above the basking rock and left on about 12 hours per day.

The addition of a small pan of water about the size of the lid of a quart mason jar and a daily change of water are good ideas. Should this dry out and be forgotten for a few days, no harm will be done. If a snake is kept in such a terrarium a dish of water large enough to accommodate the snake when it is coiled up is appreciated.

A few small potted cactuses or succulent plants add to the decor of any desert terrarium, as do a few pieces of driftwood. Neither is necessary except to please the owner's own sense of esthetics. The top of a desert terrarium may be left open if the animals are unable to climb out (and if there are no cats, dogs, or children to crawl in!). This would be the case for most lizards, but obviously not for snakes. If there is any chance of animals being able to escape, the terrarium should be covered with wire screening or some similar material that permits good air circulation. Glass covers should *not* be used in desert terrariums as they act to the disadvantage of the animals.

If a bright sunny spot is available where day air temperatures are at least 75°, the lamp need not be used. The terrarium should then be located so that direct sunlight falls upon the basking rocks for three to four hours per day. Don't forget to provide a cooler refuge in the form

The side-blotched lizard, Uta stansburiana, *is common over much of the American West. This is a small lizard with a body length of just over 2 inches. They are hardy and feed on a variety of small arthropods. In captivity, meal-worms, crickets, spiders, and flies are taken. They are also available relatively inexpensively in pet shops. Photo by F. J. Dodd, Jr.*

of deep sand and a shady rock or bark ledge under which animals may crawl.

The woodland terrarium

The woodland terrarium is quite different from the desert terrarium. In the latter we try to recreate a bit of nature that is typically hot during the day and cool at night, with very low humidity. In the former we try to recreate the floor of a deciduous forest as one finds in the New England states, for example, or in many mountains of the West. The woodland terrarium thrives best in diffuse, indirect light in a cool location. High humidity is desirable inside it. There is hardly an area in the United States where material for a woodland terrarium is not at hand—if not in near proximity, then within a short automobile drive.

Scarlet kingsnakes exist as a number of subspecies of Lampropeltis triangulum. *These stunning serpents are in great demand and thus command a high price when available. They are shy, secretive snakes that have the reputation of being rather temperamental feeders in captivity. Do not confuse these snakes with the highly venomous coral snakes, which have a similar pattern.*

The broadhead skink, Eumeces laticeps, *is an impressive animal—the adult male has a very large red head with powerful jaws and is capable of delivering a painful bite if carelessly handled. Though the body is shiny and apparently unarmored, each scale has a core of bone, and this animal has even been known to partially deflect a shotgun blast! Photo by F. J. Dodd, Jr.*

With an empty aquarium sealed against leaks, we begin the woodland terrarium by covering the bottom with a layer of coarse gravel or small pebbles to a depth of one-half to one inch. This acts as a drain to prevent the roots of plants from being immersed in water. Cover this with about 2 inches of good garden soil or, better, with soil collected from the forest or canyon floor. Into this soil are planted whatever plants we have collected. These may be mosses, ferns, lichens, liverworts, ground pine, etc. They are collected carefully, especially in the case of rooted plants such as ground pines and ferns, so that roots are not damaged. Stones already covered with moss or lichen may, if of proper size, be taken as they are, without disturbing the plants on them. In many cases, one or two such stones, a small fern or two, and some dead leaf litter are all that is needed to complete the terrarium.

One of the first harbingers of spring is this treefrog, the spring peeper, Hyla crucifer, *whose piping song can often be heard before all the snow has melted. Photo by W. Mudrack.*

If collecting your own material is difficult or uninviting, a trip to the local plant nursery can yield enough to make an attractive terrarium. In this case, cover the bottom of the aquarium with 2 to 3 inches of a good, prepared planter mix. Buy one or two small potted ferns and a small bag of sphagnum moss (sold sometimes as "green moss" or "living moss"). Plant the ferns, add a small piece of driftwood or a rock, press the moss into the soil between the ferns and the rock, and that's it. Cover with glass after having watered well enough to dampen but not soak the soil. Glass covers on top of aquarium frames usually cannot make tight seals due to slight irregularities in the frame, particularly at corners. Thus there need be no fear that animals inside will suffocate. Keep in a cool location in good light, but do not allow direct sunlight to fall onto the terrarium. Water when the soil becomes dry, as you would with a house plant. With a glass cover in place, this will probably be about once a week at the most.

This type of terrarium makes a fine home for a variety of animals, such as small toads from the garden, wood frogs (brown frogs with dark eye masks common in northeastern forests), red efts (common in the East after a rainfall), small garter snakes, ringnecked snakes, brown snakes, box turtles, spring peepers, or any of the small tree frogs common throughout the continental U.S. This kind of terrarium should not be used for anoles or aquatic turtles (too cool) or for frogs such as the pickerel frog collected in or near water (too dry). It can be easily modified for frogs by sinking a good sized glass or plastic dish into the soil and filling it with water. The dish can easily be camouflaged with small stones around its edge and a few stones in the water.

The world's largest toad is the giant toad, Bufo marinus. *This species has been widely introduced in areas far removed from its native American tropics. It was usually introduced to control insect pests, but it too became a pest because it will eat almost anything. It reaches a length of over 9 inches, so it needs a large terrarium, but is a long-lived amphibian that is easy to keep.*

Another and more permanent arrangement to accommodate frogs can be neatly made as follows. Cut a piece of glass to fit across the width of the aquarium and long enough that when an edge is placed in the bottom and the sheet is held at 45°, its upper edge is about two inches from the bottom. In a larger aquarium this can be even higher. This needn't be calculated with any great deal of accuracy; a guess will be good enough. What we are obviously going to do is construct a small pond at one end with its depth equal to the depth of the soil at the other end. The glass is propped in place with a rock or two while the aquarium is empty, and the three sides in contact with the glass are sealed with a silicone rubber compound and allowed to set. The prop can then be removed and soil, plants, etc., added to one side, some gravel and pebbles and water on the other, and we now have a kind of aqua-terrarium. Water in the pond should be changed weekly or filtered with an undergravel filter available in any tropical fish shop. In addition to aquatic frogs, such an arrangement is ideal for aquatic salamanders such as the Japanese red-bellied newt and the red-spotted newt.

The tropical terrarium

This is very similar to the foregoing and is set up in essentially the same way. Differences lie in the choice of plants. Plants used in the tropical terrarium must be those that will withstand somewhat higher temperatures and brighter light. Plants such as small philodendrons, snake plants, pothos, etc., are substituted for the ferns and ground pines of the woodland terrarium. Venus flytraps planted in small pots of peat moss or sphagnum can be placed in a tropical terrarium. Small tropical plants such as these are easily purchased in almost any market, florist, or nursery at very small cost. The tropical terrarium must be kept warm, from 75 to 85°, and part of it should either be exposed to bright daylight or illuminated by a shaded lamp bulb similar to the one used for the desert terrarium but of smaller wattage. With this increase in light and temperature the cover must be screen and not glass. The light source can be an ordinary aquarium reflector made to fit the particular aquarium being used. Screening is used to cover that part of the aquarium not covered by the reflector.

This type of terrarium is excellent for anoles ("chameleons"). If based on an aqua-terrarium as described under the woodland terrarium, the pond could house a small tropical slider turtle. A large basking rock should then be arranged so that the turtle could easily climb onto it and bask in the light of the sun or the lamp that is positioned over the rock.

Evaporation will obviously occur quite rapidly in such a terrarium, and frequent waterings of the plants will be necessary. This is best done at daily intervals with a misting bottle such as is used with house plants. Be certain to wet all leaf surfaces with this artificial rain. This is of particular importance in the case of anoles, which drink only from droplets of water caught on plants, twigs, etc.

The aqua-terrarium

Many fish fanciers combine their fish keeping with terrarium keeping in the same container, making of the combination a particularly pleasing "tropical" picture.

A somewhat more ambitious, but nonetheless easily constructed, aqua-terrarium can be made by dividing an aquarium in half by a pane of glass sealed with a silicone rubber compound. In one half an aquarium is established and in the other a tropical terrarium. At least a ten- to fifteen-gallon aquarium is best for this venture.

The back half is filled with planter mix or pebbles and soil. Tropical plants are planted in the soil, and rocks and/or driftwood is arranged to obscure the edge of the glass. The front part is covered with aquarium gravel to a depth of 1½", filled with water, and planted with such plants as *Vallisneria*, *Cryptocoryne*, *Sagittaria*, and *Ambulia*. The front aquarium half is easily heated to the 75 to 80° that most tropical fishes prefer by an aquarium heater held in place by a few small stones carefully propped against it. A small underground filter run by an inexpensive vibrator air pump will keep the aquarium water clear.

A small air pump generally has enough output to lift water an inch or two higher than the surrounding level.

Xenopus laevis is the African clawed frog, often sold in pet shops that carry tropical fishes. It is a good inhabitant for the water portion of an aqua-terrarium, but it should not be kept with small fishes, as it has a ravenous appetite. Photo by R. Zukal.

The dwarf underwater frog, Hymenochirus curtipes, *reaches only about 2 inches in length. Live tubifex worms are eagerly accepted by this species. Photo by R. Zukal.*

If the end of the return tube is bent at a right angle, it can serve as the source of a small stream spilling over a carefully arranged piece of petrified wood or shale rock positioned so that part of it is in the terrarium portion and part in the aquarium, with the water spilling directly back into the aquarium. If this can't be arranged for lack of just the right piece of rock, the tube should be cut so that it just barely breaks the water surface. Two 25-watt bulbs in the aquarium reflector or a fluorescent bulb positioned over the water will provide the light needed for both halves of the set-up. Cover the remainder with screening or glass mounted on flat sticks or cork on the frame to allow air circulation. The high temperature and humidity, plus the light, will make the arrangement ideal for anoles, tree frogs, small turtles, and aquatic salamanders plus the fish in the foreground.

Almost any kind of tropical fish can be housed in the aquarium. Platies, zebra fish, a small school of neon tetras, and young angelfish, among others, are colorful, lively, and easy to keep.

Special for turtles

Turtle hatchlings of various species (especially red-eared sliders and map turtles) were once probably the most commonly sold and abused animals kept in terraria. Here we shall confine ourselves to a discussion of a simple, easy to maintain "turtle-arium," presuming you can locate legal specimens of these species or similar ones.

The reader may have already surmised that turtles require a place to swim, warmth, and a place to crawl out and sun themselves, either in the sun or in the light from a light bulb. In addition to the two aqua-terrarium types discussed, turtles may be housed in plain aquariums, large plastic shoe boxes, or refrigerator dishes. They should be provided with a few stones arranged in stepping-stone fashion so that the highest one is completely dry and exposed to a few hours of bright sun or artificial light every day. Water should be at least 2 inches deep to allow free swimming. Since they cannot climb out over the smooth sides of an aquarium or plastic box, no cover is needed.

A three- or five-gallon aquarium can be purchased and converted into a pleasing turtle container which will ensure an adequate home for the animal. A five-gallon turtle terrarium can house up to five small turtles, though

Once sold by the millions, red-eared sliders, Pseudemys scripta elegans, *often languished under the care of ill-informed keepers.*

To heat shallow water in an aqua-terrarium, place an aquarium heater in a water-filled jar as seen here. Be careful, though, as the water in the jar will evaporate rapidly and will need to be replaced periodically.

this would be too crowded to allow much growth. Aquarium sand or gravel on the bottom, a few sprigs of elodea or cabomba, and a small potted house plant set on a rock above water line will result in an inexpensive and very pleasant to look at bit of nature. Since turtles are heavy eaters and produce a dirty aquarium, the water should be heavily filtered.

4.
Care

Plants

Some comments have already been made concerning the care of the plants in terrariums. Cacti and succulents used in the desert terrarium need watering about once a

Kingsnakes such as Lampropeltis pyromelana *usually require live rodents as food, but never leave a rodent in the cage if the snake does not attack it immediately as a rodent can seriously injure or kill a sluggish snake. Photo by Bertrand E. Baur.*

month. Water should be given them around their roots, enough to dampen but not wet the soil. These plants will not prosper if their roots are exposed to wet sand for any appreciable length of time. The light and high daytime temperatures, which are maintained primarily for the benefit of the reptiles kept in the terrarium, will at the same time contribute to the well-being of the plants.

Plants in the woodland and tropical terrariums will require more frequent watering. The soil should always be barely damp, but not wet. A guide to the proper conditions for the plants chosen for these terrariums will be the conditions under which they originally grew. Generally diffuse light and cooler temperatures are best for ferns, mosses, ground pines, and similar woodland plants, with slightly brighter light and warmer temperatures for the tropical plants. Woodland terrariums do best at temperatures below 70°, tropical terrariums above this temperature. A 10° fluctuation above for tropical and below for woodland is well within the limits tolerated by both the plants and animals selected for each terrarium.

Animals

The proper care of commonly available terrarium animals is quite simple. Recognizing the fact that our terrarium cannot maintain an optimum body temperature except within relatively narrow environmental limits, we must provide an environment in which this need is provided for. Knowledge of temperature requirements is of primary importance in keeping reptiles and, to a somewhat lesser extent, amphibians.

Terrarium animals have differing food requirements. This is somewhat at variance with experience gained

Well-known to many amateur herp collectors are the garter snakes of the genus Thamnophis. *These are probably the perfect snakes for the beginner. They are easily collected (or can be cheaply purchased), and they will feed eagerly on earthworms, small fishes, frogs, and the like. Be sure not to keep them too moist, however, or they will develop unsightly boils from fungal infections. Though they may release an unpleasant musk when first captured, they usually tame easily and soon abandon this habit. Photo of* Thamnophis marcianus *by Ken Lucas, Steinhart Aquarium.*

with tropical fishes for which commercially available dried food diets are easily obtained and meet the needs of most aquarium inhabitants. In order to keep reptiles and amphibians properly one must know, in addition,to temperature requirements, something about the type of food each kind of reptile or amphibian normally requires.

Vertical pupils on lidless eyes mark the Tokay Gecko.
Photo by H. Hansen, Aquarium Berlin.

5.
Desert Reptiles

Desert reptiles require a dry environment with relatively high daytime temperatures and cool night temperatures. In addition, most require direct sunshine with access to cooler shade or artificial sunshine provided by incandes-

A beautiful male collared lizard, Crotaphytus collaris. *When alarmed, this lizard can run on its hind legs, looking for all the world like a little* Tyrannosaurus. *Photo by Aaron Norman.*

Although frequently offered for sale, horned lizards of the genus Phrynosoma *make very poor pets. They need to be kept very hot and very dry, and they feed almost exclusively on massive quantities of ants. Most decline rapidly and die in captivity. Photo by Ken Lucas, Steinhart Aquarium.*

cent lamps (not fluorescent, which is too cool). A pile of small rocks directly under the lamp or placed to receive three to four hours of direct sun per day is easily arranged. If a fairly large rock is positioned under a bright, shaded light bulb so that the rock area directly below the lamp becomes almost too hot to comfortably keep a hand on but the edges of the rock are away from the lamp and cool, an ideal situation is created wherein the reptiles can seek out that part of the rock on which they can get the heat and light they need. By moving on and off and closer and further from the edge, they will automatically adjust their temperature to their own operating optimum. Air temperature in the shady, cooler position of the terrarium should be around 75 to 85°F during the day, and 70 to 80°F during the night. Warmer temperatures during the night are most harmful.

Fence lizards or swifts (*Sceloporus* and relatives)

These are the most commonly kept desert reptiles and are generally familiar even to the eastern terrarium keeper. These lizards prosper very well in the desert terrarium as described. They should be fed at least two to three times per week with living insects that are large enough for them to swallow, since they do not chew their food. The ideal and most easily obtainable food for these animals is mealworms, which are available in many pet shops or in bait shops, where they may be sold as "golden worms." Enough worms should be fed at one feeding so that the animals are satisfied and ignore any additional worms. During the summer, when night temperatures are likely to be higher, more food will be taken than during the winter. It should be dropped directly in front of the reptile and must be alive and moving. In addition to mealworms, such insects as

A swift, Sceloporus orcutti. *Photo by Aaron Norman.*

beetles, grasshoppers, and crickets are eaten. Flies are generally too fast for most swifts. The wider the variety of insects fed the less chance of digestive problems—a diet of only mealworms may eventually cause intestinal disorders.

Some people fill a small porcelain dish, such as a canary bird bath, with an excess of mealworms in a bit of the material in which they are sold and leave this dish constantly in the terrarium. This is an excellent way to provide food whenever it is needed.

Swifts and similar lizards are commonly available in most areas and from various commercial sources.

Chuckwallas (*Sauromalus*)

This is one of the largest North American lizards. In its native habitat it lives in and among large rocks into which it can retreat when threatened. It can inflate itself to such a degree that it can rarely be extracted by a man tugging on a leg or tail. Though not colorful, this animal makes an excellent pet and can be easily tamed to the point where it will move expectantly toward the front of the terrarium upon the approach of its owner and will feed from his hand. Some individuals become so tame that they must be restrained from climbing onto the owner's hand and up his sleeve looking for food. This they do by constantly flicking out their tongue to taste the hand and sleeve.

Since the chuckwalla grows to over a foot in length, it must be kept in a large terrarium. Despite its large and, to some people, formidable appearance, this lizard is primarily a vegetarian. In its southwestern desert home it gorges itself on the small annual plants that carpet the

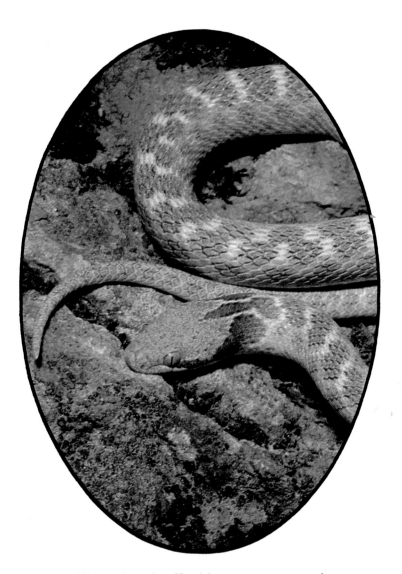

Night snakes such as Hypsiglena torquata *are somewhat difficult to keep, as they feed mostly on lizards. They are mildly venomous but are not considered to be a threat to humans. Photo by Ken Lucas, Steinhart Aquarium.*

desert floor for a few weeks each spring and on the leaves and fruit of the sparse shrubs and some cacti during the rest of the warm season. After late summer and during the winter, food for this animal is quite scarce and it lives on reserves of flesh and fat in its large tail. In the terrarium it feeds readily on lettuce, lawn clippings, dandelion leaves, and small bits of banana, and it particularly likes yellow flowers such as dandelions and some lilies. A few mealworms once a week are also relished.

The desert iguana, Dipsosaurus dorsalis, *is a hardy vegetarian from the Sonora Desert. This lizard becomes quite tame and will often take food from its owner's hand. Photo by J. K. Langhammer.*

Desert iguana (*Dipsosaurus*)

This large lizard has feeding habits much like the chuckawalla and can be fed the same way. It lives on the open desert, hiding from excess heat during the day under the bushes and in rodent burrows. It tolerates tem-

The chuckwalla or chuckawalla, Sauromalus obesus. *Most herpetologists today prefer the use of the name "chuckwalla" over the older "chuckawalla." This large desert lizard is primarily a vegetarian and is especially fond of yellow flowers. It is capable of inflating its body to wedge itself into a crevice when alarmed. When so anchored it is almost impossible to remove. Photo by J. K. Langhammer.*

peratures in excess of 100°F and in the wild may be found abroad when most other reptiles have retreated from the heat of the day. In the terrarium it prefers large sandy areas, a basking rock, and perhaps a piece of driftwood to climb on.

Collared lizards (*Crotaphytus*)

One or another species or subspecies of the collared lizard is found in rocky desert and semi-desert throughout most of the western U.S. and they are commonly available in dealers' stocks in larger cities. These beautiful animals are primarily carnivorous, feeding in nature on almost anything moving that is small enough to be captured and swallowed. This includes other lizards as well as insects. For this reason they cannot be housed in a terrarium with other lizards unless they are at least of equal size. They will thrive on grasshoppers, crickets, and mealworms. If small fence lizards are easily obtained they may also be fed to collared lizards.

Tortoises

Young tortoises are occasionally offered for sale. Some of these are imported from the Old World and very closely resemble our own American species. **American species are protected by law and though easily captured should be left alone if encountered on the desert.** Desert tortoises may be confused with box turtles and consequently improperly housed. The desert forms may be recognized by their thick, untapered stubby legs with no apparent "wrist"; they cannot "close up" like box turtles. Desert tortoises should be kept on sand and provided with a dish of drinking water. Their food consists of watery plant material such as suggested for chuckawallas and desert iguanas. There is a very high mortality rate among tortoises kept by hobbyists, and they can be recommended only for specialists or advanced hobbyists.

Banded geckos (*Coleonyx*)

Geckos are a lizard group commonly represented throughout the tropics of the world. These tropical forms generally have suction pads on their toes and use them for climbing trees and walls to feed on insects. The banded gecko (and the few other similar species) of the American deserts is a small, nocturnal relative of these tropical forms. It lacks suction pads. Unlike most desert lizards it completely avoids the heat of the day by hiding under debris, rocks, or in rodent burrows. As a consequence it is easy to keep in captivity. It will shun a lamp and direct sun, so these should not be provided. Daytime temperatures between 70 to 80°F suit it well. If no hiding place under a rock is provided and the animal is kept in the shade, it will always be walking about its terrarium. A two- or five-gallon tank with one-half inch of fine sand and a bit of driftwood is all it needs. This is one of the few reptiles capable of sound production other than a hiss. Some tropical geckos bark when disturbed; the banded gecko will make a kind of squeaky "Eh!". Feed them on mealworms and similar insects.

Snakes

Snakes are found in deserts, woodlands, swamps, rain forests—in short, in most kinds of habitats in the temperate and tropical world. Despite this, snakes in general may be easily housed in a modified desert terrarium. This should include a sandy or loose soil floor, a dish of water large enough to accommodate the coiled-

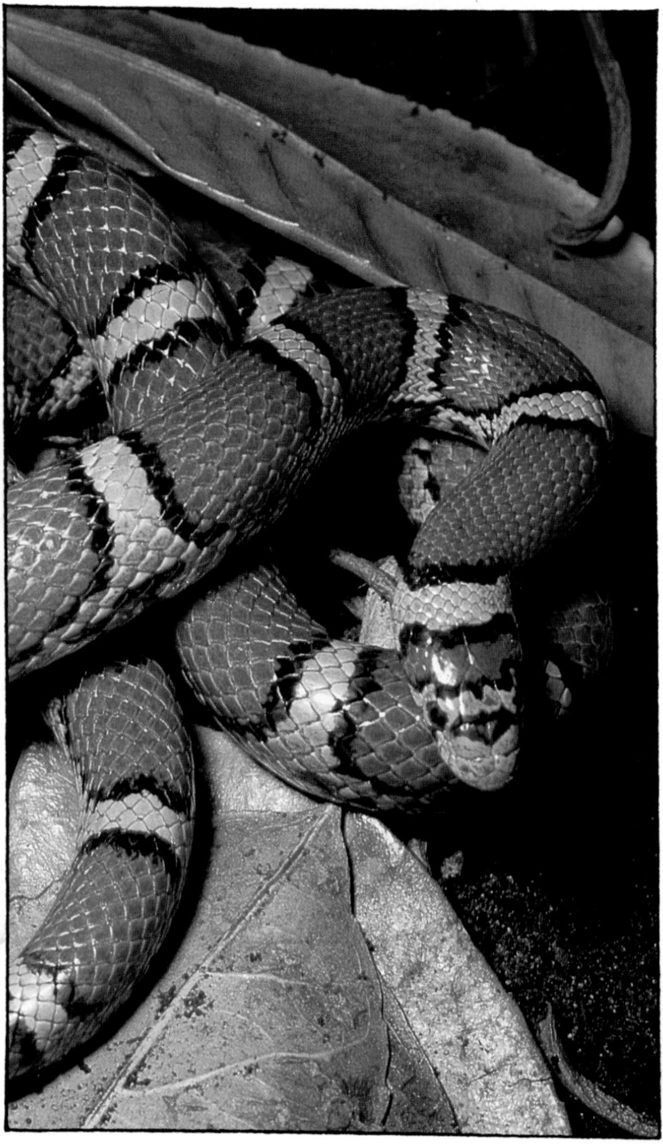

up snake, and a stick or two so arranged that the snake can climb onto it and coil up on it. Some species will seek out shelter under a rock or piece of bark on the terrarium floor. Some snake keepers provide a piece of burlap large enough for the snake to hide under. Temperatures should be kept between 70 to 80°F during the day. A lamp or direct sun is appreciated but should always be arranged so that cooler areas are available. Water in the dish should be changed daily.

All snakes are carnivores. For smaller snakes such as ringnecked or brown snakes, mealworms, grasshoppers, and crickets are generally sufficient. Newly-born mice are taken by smaller snakes. King snakes will eat small lizards as well as small mice. Brown snakes and a few others like earthworms. Water snakes feed on fresh fish such as a freshly killed goldfish, small frogs and toads, and occasionally on mice. Larger snakes such as bull snakes, milk snakes, and boas of all sorts feed almost exclusively on small mammals (rats, mice) and birds (baby chicks, etc.), preferably live. Many snakes will accept a freshly killed or frozen and thawed food animal. Large boas in zoos are fed on large rats or rabbits, generally after the zoo closes at night. Snakes of the constricting type generally kill their food animals by holding on with their teeth to some part of the animal while wrapping their bodies tightly around it and asphyxiating it. Death is generally swift. After killing the prey the snake eats it whole. This is possible even with prey much larger in diameter than the snake because of its specialized jaw suspension that makes it possible for snakes to enlarge their mouth capacity to many times

Yet another of the seemingly infinite variations of Lamropeltis triangulum, *the red milk snake,* L. t. syspila. *Photo by Ken Lucas, Steinhart Aquarium.*

the normal size. Fur, feathers, and bone are not digested and pass through the snake's digestive tract. Consequently, the snake's cage must be cleaned frequently.

Garter snakes will usually take earthworms. Some enterprising herpetologists mix live earthworms with hamburger. By gradually reducing the number of worms they teach the snake to eat meat. Water snakes can often be induced to eat strips of fish that are cut into fish shapes. With threads attached to simulate movement, the snakes take them readily.

Snakes generally require food only once a week. If kept at the proper temperature, a large or growing snake may feed twice a week. If it ignores food animals on which it has previously fed, the food should be withdrawn and tried again in a week. Snakes can survive in fair health for many weeks or even months without feeding, though the stress may lead to diseases. An occasional specimen may refuse to eat at all in captivity and may have to be force-fed. Force-feeding is traumatic and somewhat dangerous to the snake and is best not attempted by the beginner. A non-feeding snake should be returned to where it was caught if local or to the pet shop if purchased. A recently fed snake should never be handled, as this may induce it to regurgitate its meal. Digestion is in part dependent on the snake's temperature, and for this reason, after being fed snakes should be kept in at least 75°F.

6.
Woodland Reptiles

Anoles *(Anolis)* (American chameleons)

These interesting little lizards are very common in the southeastern United States and Caribbean region. They are not true chameleons, which are limited to an Old

An American "chameleon," Anolis carolinensis, the green anole. Photo by G. Marcuse.

True chameleons are slow-moving arboreal lizards from the Old World. They are insect-eaters with fantastic projectile tongues. They have opposable digits and prehensile tails, and many are highly adorned. This is a male Jackson's chameleon, Chameleo jacksoni. *It has been remarked this lizard bears a strong superficial resemblance to the extinct horned dinosaur* Triceratops. *Although interesting and distinctive, chameleons seldom survive long in captivity, though the reasons for this are poorly known. Photo by J. Bridges.*

An attractive garter snake is the California red-sided garter snake, Thamnophis sirtalis infernalis. *Photo by Ken Lucas, Steinhart Aquarium.*

World distribution and which are quite different animals. Stories of their ability to change color to match their background are exaggerated. Anoles are capable of color changes from green to brown and vice-versa but cannot match reds, blues, or checkerboard patterns. Color change in the anole is relatively slow and in part dependent on temperature. When cold or ill they are generally brown; when warm and well-fed, usually green.

Anoles should be kept in tropical terrariums with green growing plants at temperatures of 75 to 85°F. They live very well in the tropical aqua-terrariums described earlier. Anoles require frequent drinks, which are obtained primarily from droplets on the terrarium glass or on the leaves of plants. Daily spraying of the plant leaves with a mister will assure that the animals get enough to drink.

Their food is insects. In captivity they feed well on mealworms dropped near them, small crickets, grasshoppers, and flies.

If keeping the anole terrarium warm enough poses a problem, it can be met by purchasing a small aquarium heater from a pet shop. This heater is then immersed in a quart jar of water set in place in the terrarium. Once plugged in, the device will maintain the proper temperature in the terrarium. Care must be exercised to keep the jar filled with water as the heater will induce rapid evaporation. Should the water level drop too low there is danger that the heater tube will crack.

Anoles are quite different from chameleons. This is the Jamaican giant anole, Anolis garmani. Photo by J. Bridges.

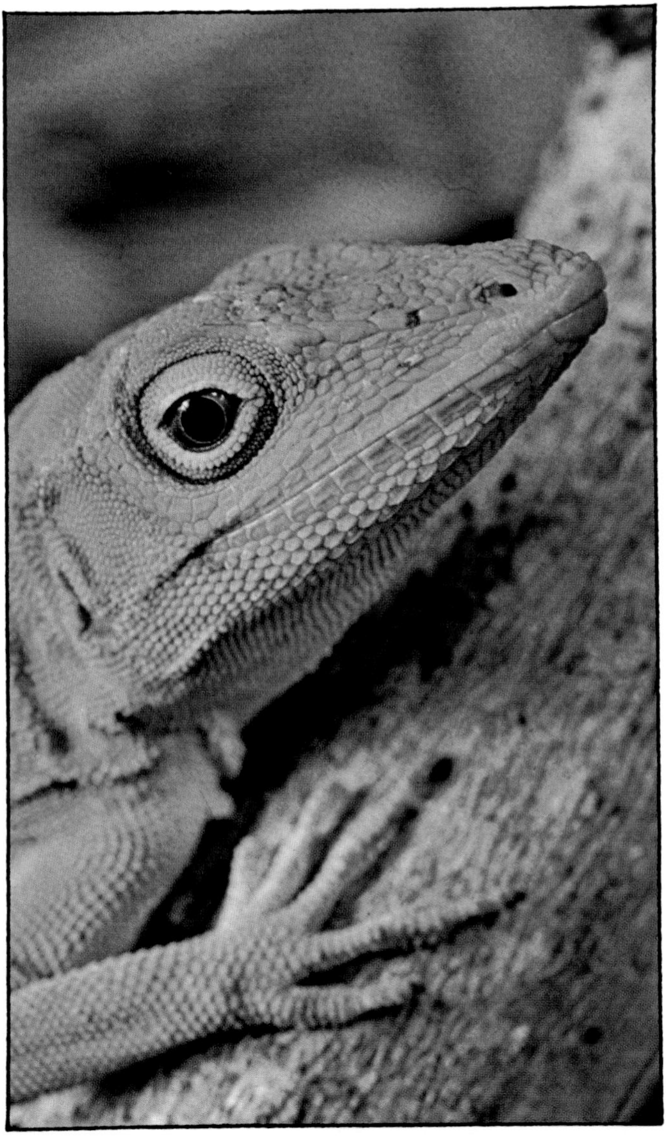

Iguanas *(Iguana)*

These large green, tree-living lizards are native to tropical America, and young ones are often sold in pet shops in the U.S. They should be housed in tropical terrariums much as anoles, with the addition of a large branched stick on which they can climb. Iguanas are primarily vegetarians and will eat most plants in the terrarium. For this reason live plants may be left out or plastic ones substituted. It is important, however, to keep the terrarium warm with high humidity and provided with climbing branches. Food for the iguana consists of lettuce, peeled bananas, yellow flowers, bits of tomato, and cut-up apple. Food may be placed in a crotch of the branches or in a small pan on the terrarium floor. Adult iguanas reach a length of 5 to 6 feet and are prized as food in Mexico.

Iguana iguana, the green iguana. This is a large jungle lizard that will eat many kinds of leaves and fruits. Do not feed it only lettuce, as this diet has no nutritional value! Photo by J. Dommers.

Mississippi map turtle, Graptemys kohni, *Photo by Tom Caravaglia.*

Turtles

Small aquatic turtles can no longer be legally sold in the U.S. because of health codes, but they are readily captured in some areas. Adult turtles of several types are often seen for sale.

Hatchling turtles should be housed in containers with at least 3 to 4 inches of water and with some rocks so arranged that the turtle can crawl out into the sun or under the lamp to sun itself. Opportunities for sunning are very important, and lack of sun is one of the chief causes of the condition of soft shell, which will eventually kill the animal. Though turtles in their natural habitat range far into the cooler parts of the U.S. and in nature some hibernate under the ice of winter, in captivity they should be kept warm at between 75 to 85°F. This is easily accomplished by the use of a small, inexpensive aquarium heater in the water.

Box turtles such as this Terrapene carolina *may be let outdoors periodically, but will escape with surprising speed if left unwatched for even a little while. Photo by Dr. Herbert R. Axelrod.*

Young turtles have very good appetites when kept properly warm. Water in their terrarium should be changed at least twice weekly, the old water being poured, dipped or siphoned out and fresh tap water of the same temperature used as replacement. If a heater is used, be certain to unplug it before draining the terrarium. Filtration with a power filter or corner filters is strongly recommended.

Aquatic turtles will quickly dirty the water in their closed terrarium, so filters or frequent water changes are an absolute necessity. Shown is Pseudemys concinna.

A few sprigs of some inexpensive aquarium plant such as elodea or cabomba will make the turtle aqua-terrarium more attractive and will provide the small amount of plant material the turtles eat. The major food of baby turtles is meat in one form or another. Small pieces of lean beef (beef heart is excellent) and bits of fish cut to about the size of a pea are easy to obtain and are among the best foods. Freshly swatted flies, mealworms, and bits of earthworm are also excellent. Turtles should be given what they will eat within an hour and any excess must be removed. People who have aquariums in addition to terrariums may feed turtles on the excess of crushed baby snails. Feedings should be daily, but periods of a week or two with no food will do little harm. Aquatic turtles can only feed under water.

If properly fed, kept in clean water between 75 to 85°F, and given an opportunity for a daily sun bath, there are very few diseases the captive baby turtle will contract. Soft shell and fungused eyes, the two most common turtle diseases, occur after prolonged abuse. Medications for these conditions are available in pet shops, but since their prevention is much easier than their cure, the reader is advised to set up the turtle terrarium properly at the outset and thus avoid these problems.

Box turtles and similar terrestrial turtles should be housed in woodland terrariums with a dish of drinking water. Sun is not necessary, though some terrestrial turtles do like to bask. As they usually are omnivorous, food consists of earthworms, mealworms, bits of raw lean beef, sow or pill bugs, grasshoppers and similar fare, as well as fresh fruits and vegetables. A piece of fresh lettuce or cut-up tomato, apple, banana, berries, peaches, etc., once or twice a week is advisable.

Caimans

Most caimans available in pet shops are shipped up as hatchlings from South America. This traffic has been largely curtailed. Spectacled caimans are occasionally imported, but their sale is usually strictly controlled in most states. Actually, caimans make poor pets for the beginning hobbyist.

Dracaena guianensis is a teiid known as the "caiman lizard." Do not confuse it with the true caiman, which is a crocodilian. Photo by H. Hansen, Aquarium Berlin.

Caimans are tropical animals. They must be kept warm if they are to survive and thrive. They should be housed in a terrarium as described for turtles, but since caimans are larger animals their terrariums must also be larger. A ten-gallon aquarium is too small for a small caiman.

Caimans take their food at the surface or on their basking areas. They should be fed on fresh fish or lean meat dropped onto their basking rock or held with tongs at the surface until they snap it up. Food should not be dropped into the water. Live goldfish may be fed to them, and they will catch them when they are hungry. If well-fed and warm, a hatchling caiman will double its size in about a year. The water must be kept very clean, basking must be available at all times, and vitamin supplements are strongly advocated.

Caiman crocodilus is usually mean-tempered and makes a poor pet. Even if well-maintained (which they seldom are), they grow much too large for a home hobbyist to deal with. Photo by Aaron Norman.

7.
Amphibians

Frogs, toads, and salamanders

Amphibians lack scales, and without this protection against water loss they are (with few exceptions) obliged to remain in or near water or damp places. They may

Poison-arrow frogs such as Dendrobates quinquevittatus *are very popular, but their skin secretions are extremely venomous, so handle with care! Photo courtesy Dr. D. Terver, Nancy Aquarium, France.*

Newts such as the crested newt, Triturus cristatus, *are delightful subjects for study in an aqua-terrarium, and as an added bonus, are fairly easy to breed in captivity.*

be housed in either woodland terrariums or aqua-terrariums and kept cool at temperatures between 60 to 70°F; tropical species need somewhat warmer temperatures.

Of these amphibians, toads are the least dependent on water. A damp woodland terrarium suits them best. Most toads will dig backwards with their hind legs into the soil and remain buried most of the day, coming out to feed at night. If the soil is kept barely damp and shallow, they cannot completely hide and will be more easily seen. The best foods for toads are earthworms and larger insects such as grasshoppers. They will also eat mealworms. It is fairly easy to teach a toad to take bits of meat suspended from a string jiggled to attract its attention. Frogs may be fed this way also. The secret is to make the food appear alive by moving it. The warty skin of toads secretes a substance that is irritating to the eyes and mouth of a potential predator. A dog or cat will quickly drop a toad it has picked up. After handling a toad the hands should be carefully washed to avoid possible irritation to the eyes should the hands be brought into contact with them. Stories about toads causing warts on the hand of a person handling them are without any foundation.

Tree frogs, especially tropical species, make excellent pets. They usually need moist aqua-terrariums with climbing branches. Small flies are excellent food.

Frogs require water and a bit of land to hop out onto. On land they feed on worms and insects. Large frogs, such as the bullfrog and horned frogs, may feed on small mice and other, smaller species of frogs.

Mealworms should be fed cautiously to frogs, as there have been cases where living mealworms have literally chewed their way through a frog's stomach, causing death. To be on the safe side, it is probably best not to feed mealworms to smaller frogs.

There are many species of salamanders in the U.S. The majority are found in damp woodland areas under logs, rocks, and leaf debris. In general, salamanders should be housed in damp, cool woodland terrariums and fed with small insects and small earthworms. Whiteworms sold in tropical fish shops are excellent food. A few commonly available salamanders may be housed in unheated aquariums set up as described for turtles. These are the Japanese red-bellied newt (*Cynops pyrrhogaster*), the Pacific newts (*Taricha*), and the eastern spotted newt (*Notophthalmus viridescens*).

These three newts will feed best underwater on tubifex worms, raw beef or fish cut to proper size, and small earthworms fed daily. As is commonly the case with most herptiles, periods of a week or two without food will cause no problem though they should be avoided if possible. The common red eft of the East is the juvenile of the spotted newt. It should be kept in woodland terrariums, being unable to survive in water until its second or third year.